Beginning Piano Solo

THE MOST BEAUTIFUL SONGS EVER

T0084196

The following songs are the property of:

Bourne Co.
Music Publishers
5 West 37th Street
New York, NY 10018

Here's That Rainy Day
In the Wee Small Hours of the Morning
Smile
Some Day My Prince Will Come

ISBN 978-1-4768-7560-6

HAL•LEONARD®
CORPORATION

7777 W. BLUEMOUND RD. P.O. BOX 13819 MILWAUKEE, WI 53213

Visit Hal Leonard Online at
www.halleonard.com

AN AFFAIR TO REMEMBER

(Our Love Affair)

from AN AFFAIR TO REMEMBER

Words by HAROLD ADAMSON
and LEO McCAREY
Music by HARRY WARREN

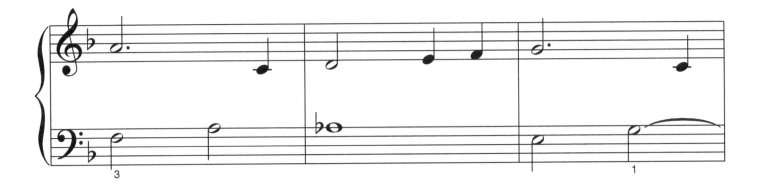

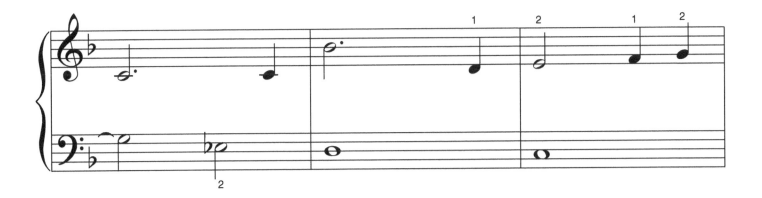

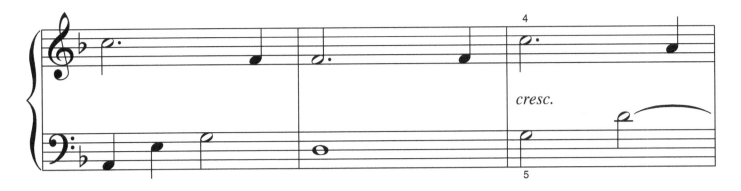

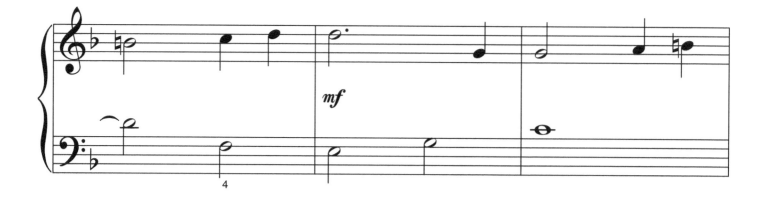

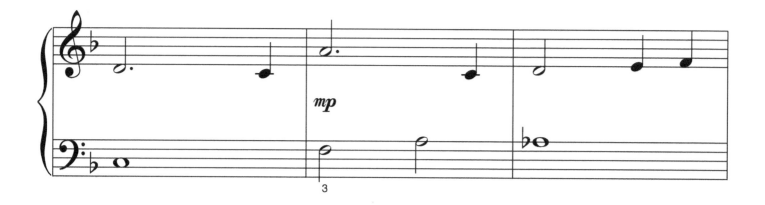

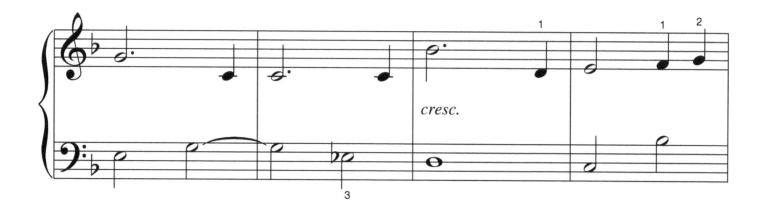

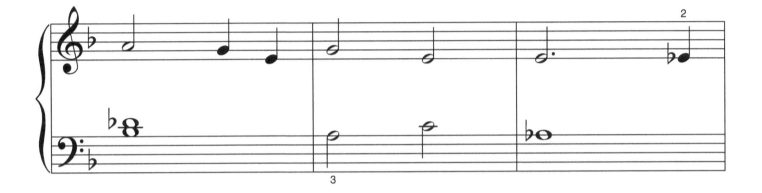

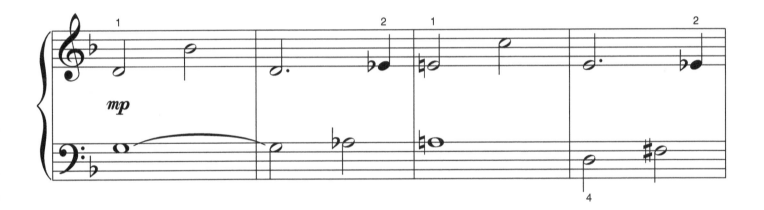

All the Things You Are

from VERY WARM FOR MAY

Lyrics by OSCAR HAMMERSTEIN II
Music by JEROME KERN

Moderately

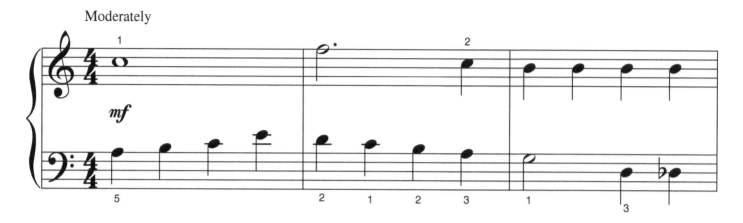

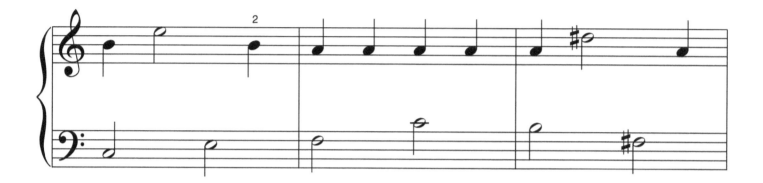

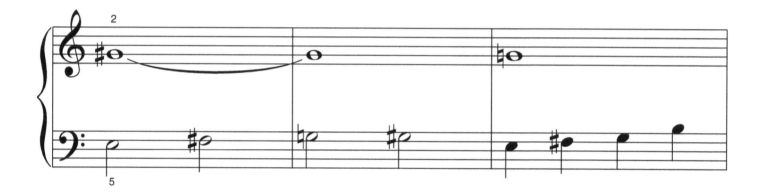

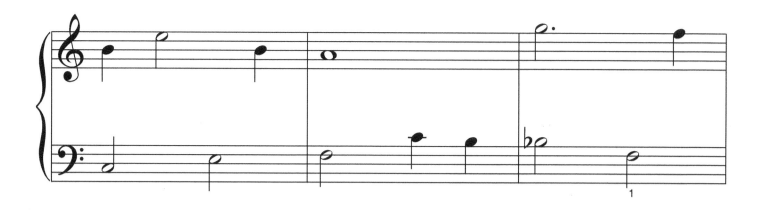

BEWITCHED
from PAL JOEY

Words by LORENZ HART
Music by RICHARD RODGERS

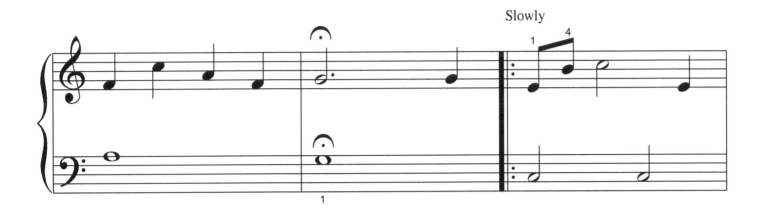

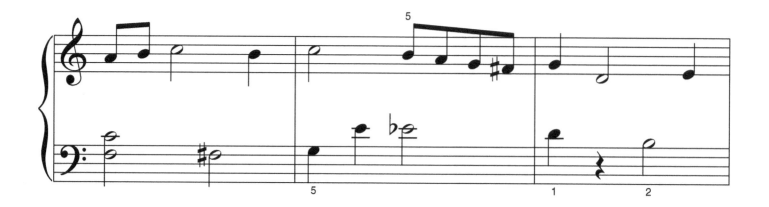

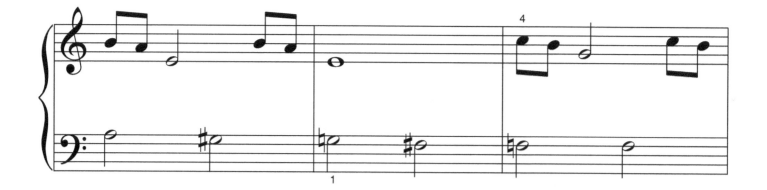

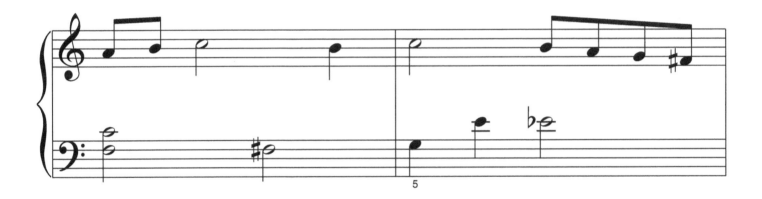

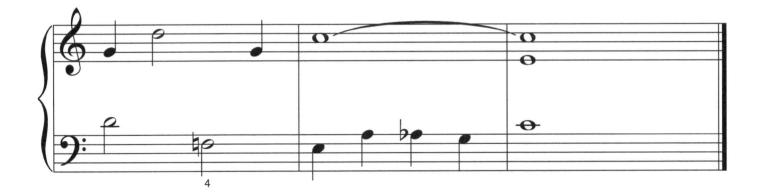

BODY AND SOUL

Words and Music by EDWARD HEYMAN,
ROBERT SOUR and FRANK EYTON
Music by JOHN GREEN

Slowly

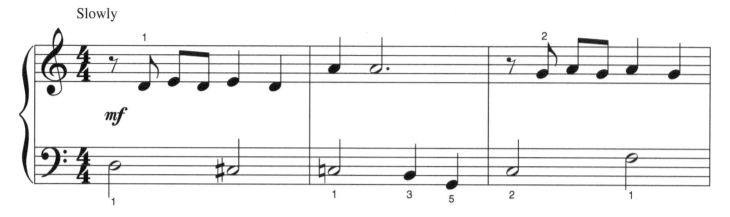

CLIMB EV'RY MOUNTAIN
from THE SOUND OF MUSIC

Lyrics by OSCAR HAMMERSTEIN II
Music by RICHARD RODGERS

Moderately slow

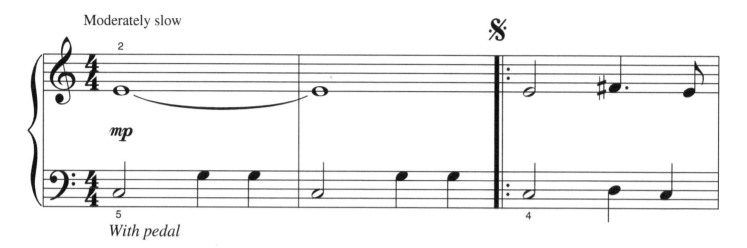

With pedal

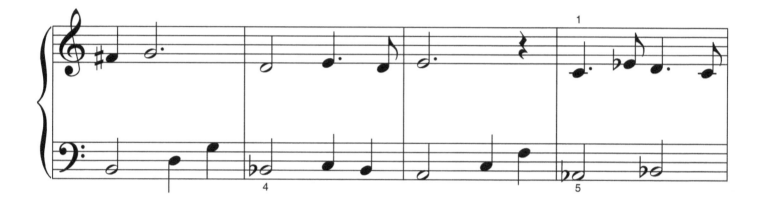

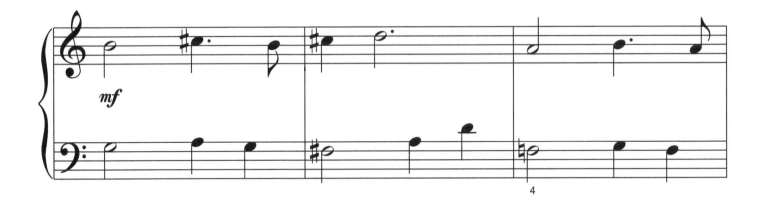

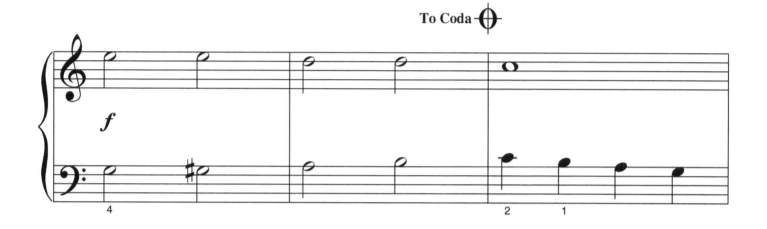

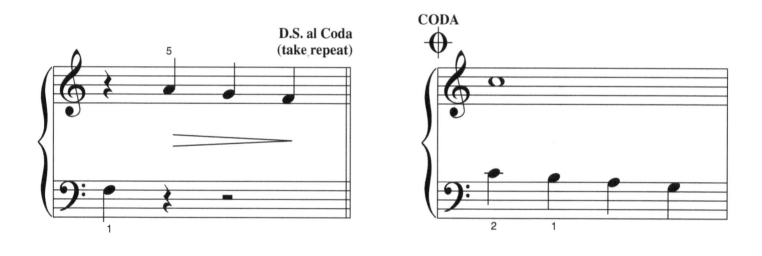

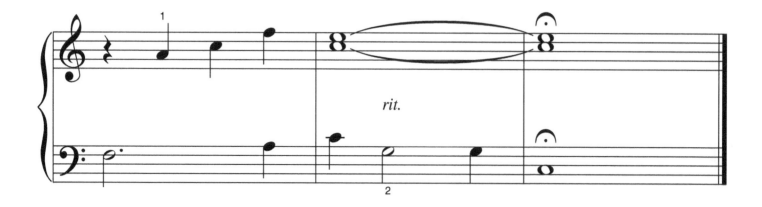

ENDLESS LOVE

Words and Music by
LIONEL RICHIE

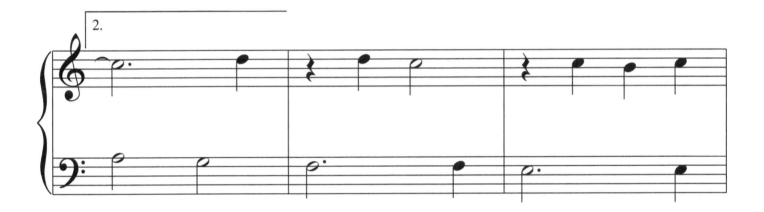

DAYS OF WINE AND ROSES
from DAYS OF WINE AND ROSES

Lyrics by JOHNNY MERCER
Music by HENRY MANCINI

Moderately slow

With pedal

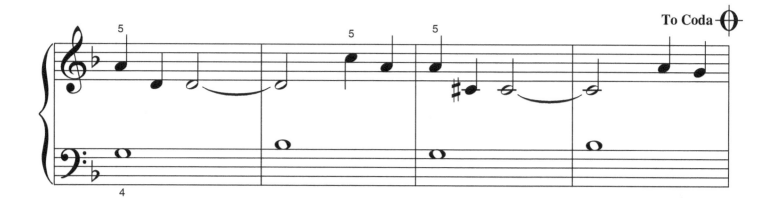

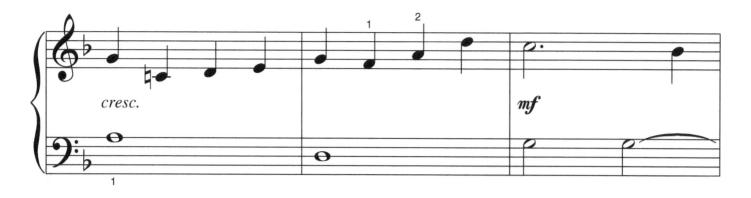

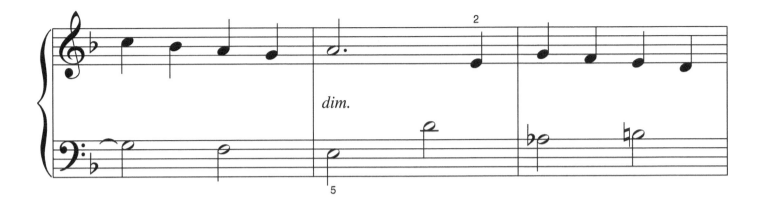

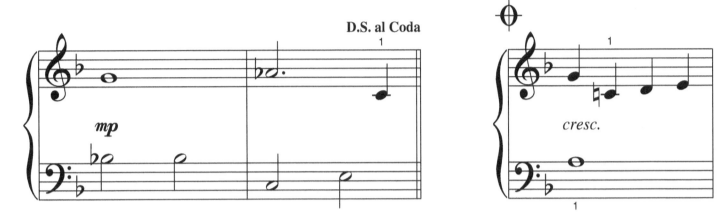

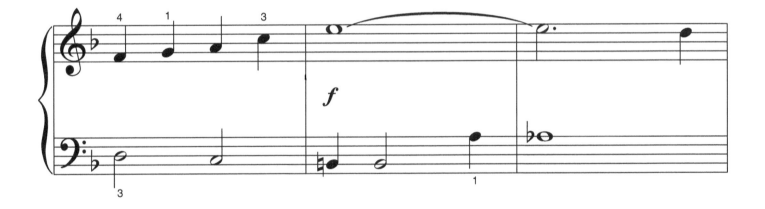

DREAM

Words and Music by
JOHNNY MERCER

Slowly

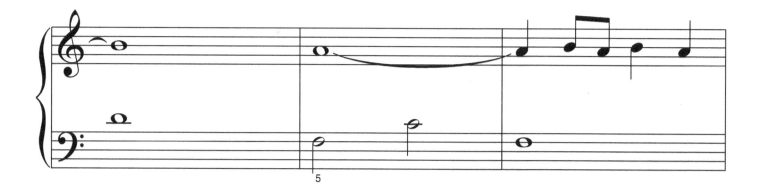

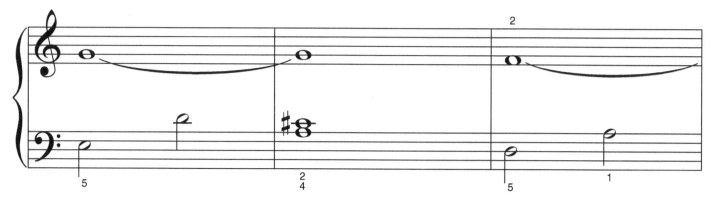

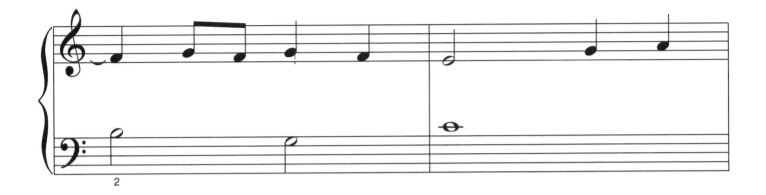

A DREAM IS A WISH YOUR HEART MAKES

from Walt Disney's CINDERELLA

Words and Music by MACK DAVID,
AL HOFFMAN and JERRY LIVINGSTON

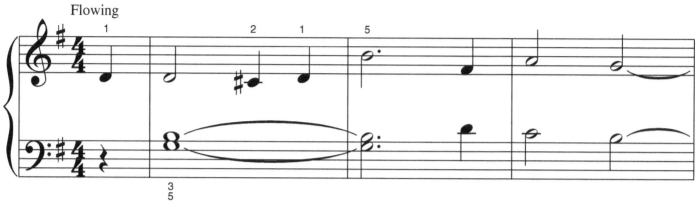

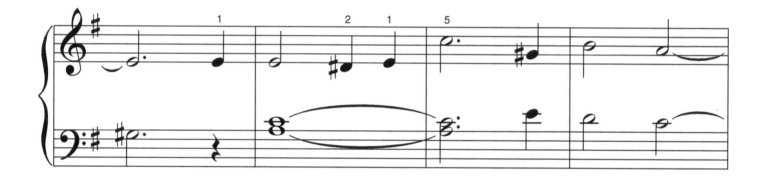

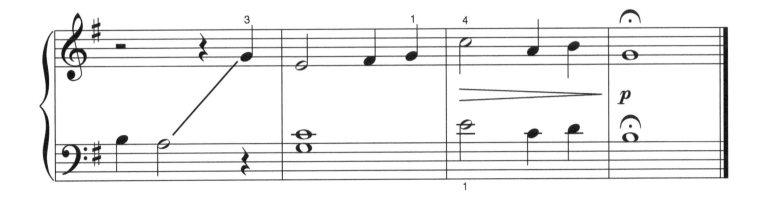

GEORGIA ON MY MIND

Words by STUART GORRELL
Music by HOAGY CARMICHAEL

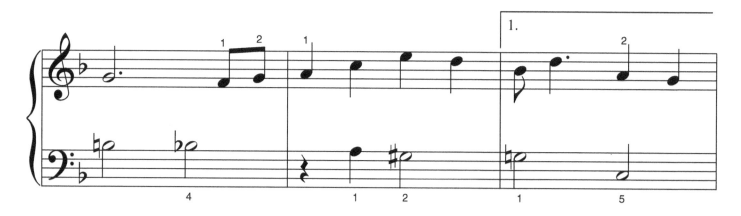

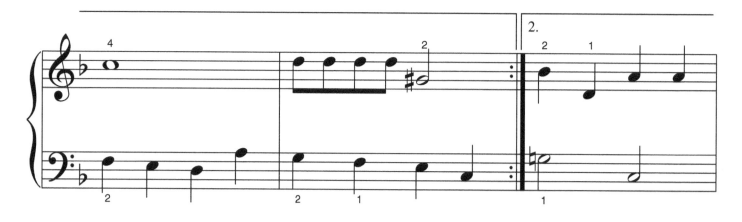

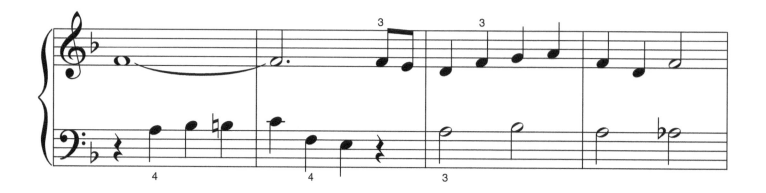

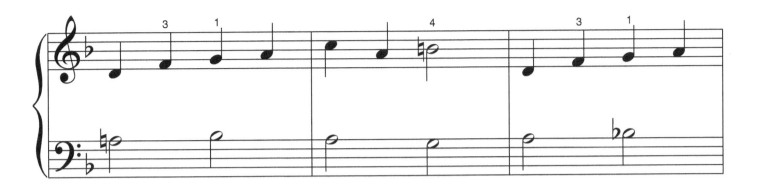

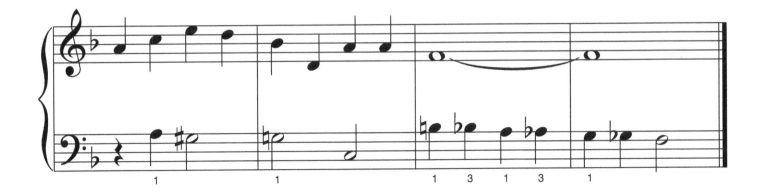

GOOD NIGHT

Words and Music by JOHN LENNON
and PAUL McCARTNEY

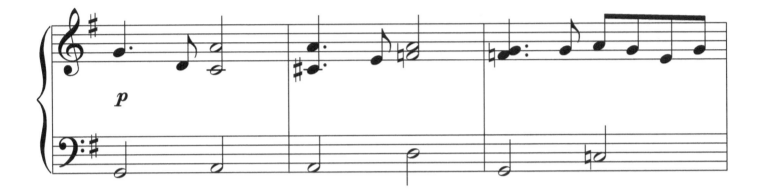

HERE'S THAT RAINY DAY
from CARNIVAL IN FLANDERS

Words by JOHNNY BURKE
Music by JIMMY VAN HEUSEN

Slowly

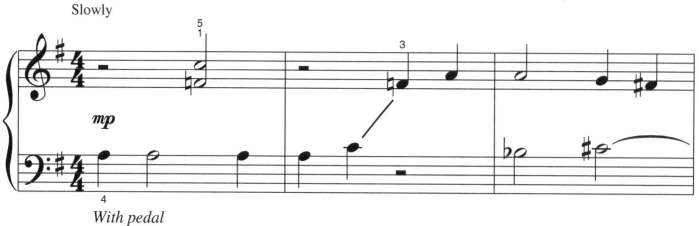

With pedal

To Coda

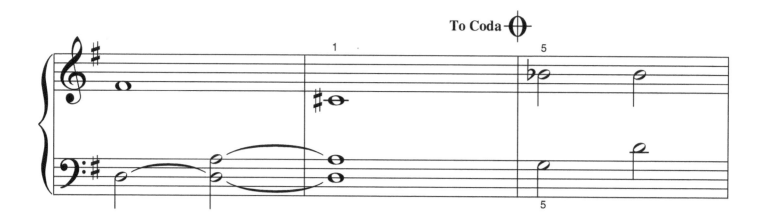

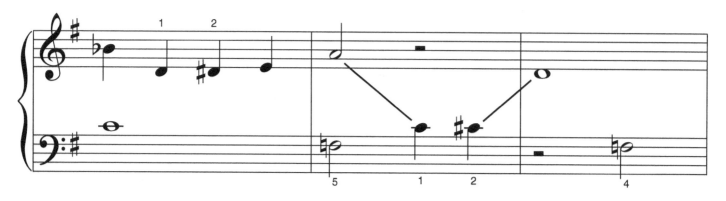

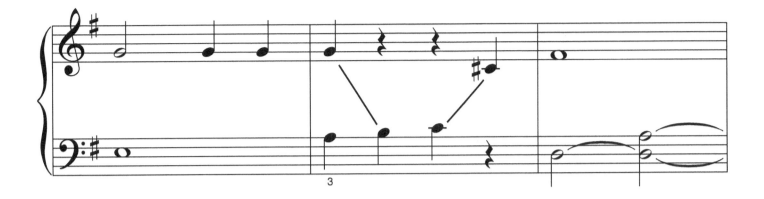

D.C. al Coda

CODA

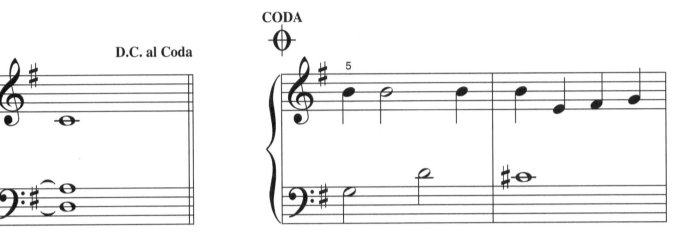

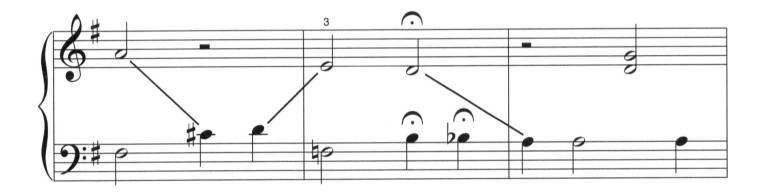

HOW ARE THINGS IN GLOCCA MORRA

from Finian's Rainbow

Words by E.Y. "YIP" HARBURG
Music by BURTON LANE

Slowly

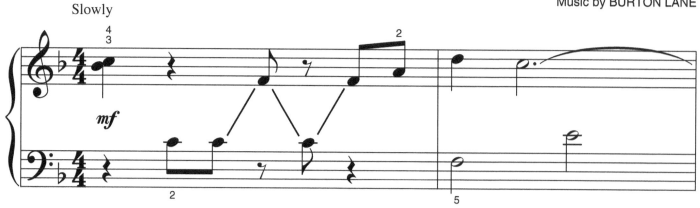

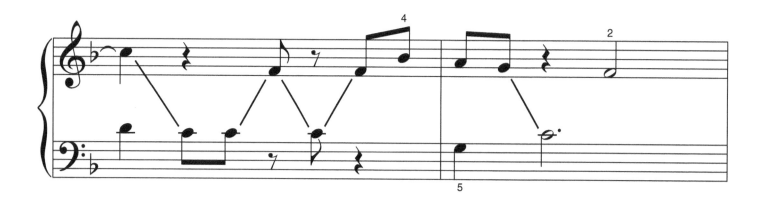

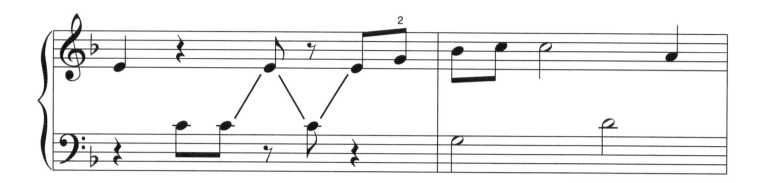

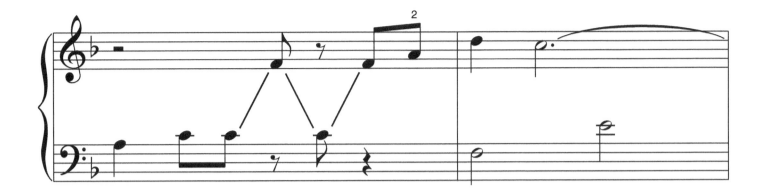

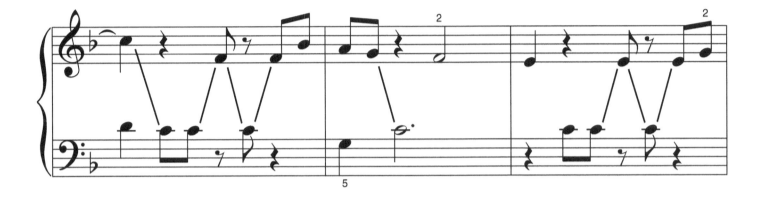

I'LL REMEMBER APRIL

Words and Music by PAT JOHNSTON,
DON RAYE and GENE DE PAUL

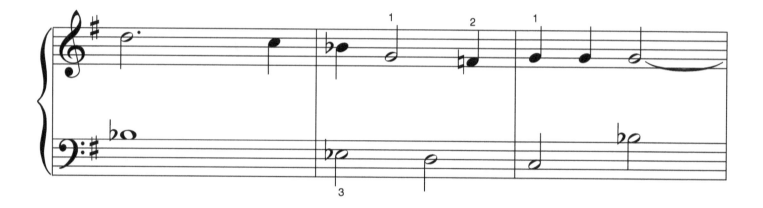

D.C. al Coda

CODA

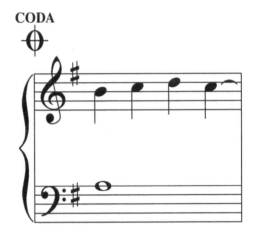

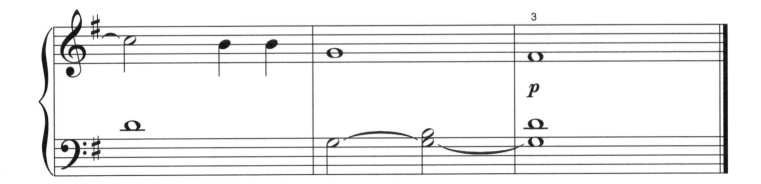

HOW DEEP IS THE OCEAN
(How High Is the Sky)

Words and Music by
IRVING BERLIN

Moderately

With pedal

To Coda

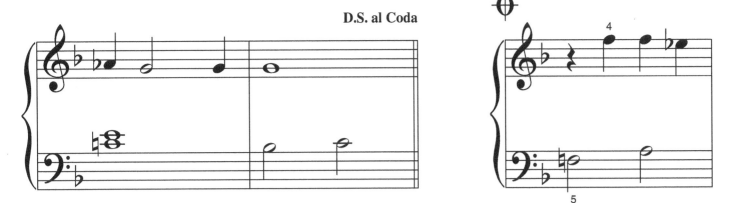

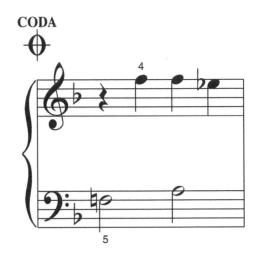

D.S. al Coda

CODA

I LEFT MY HEART IN SAN FRANCISCO

Words by DOUGLASS CROSS
Music by GEORGE CORY

Slowly

mp

With pedal

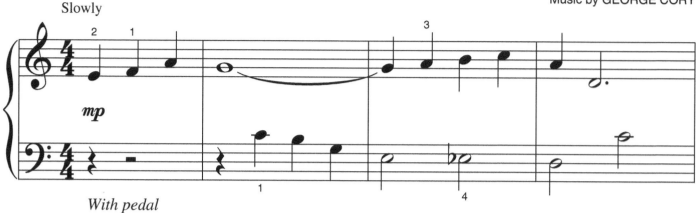

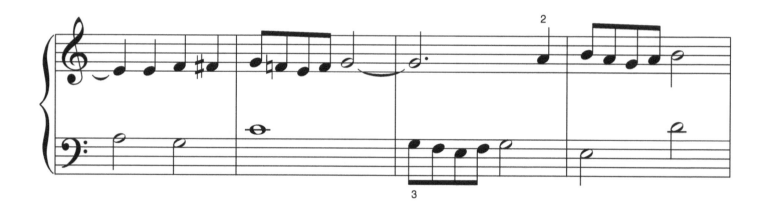

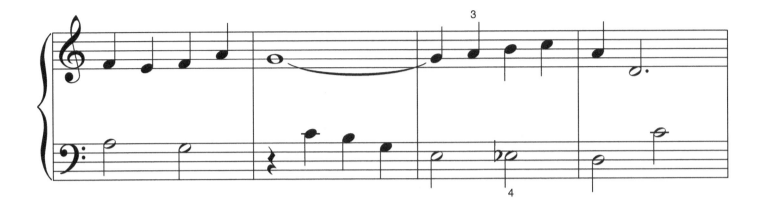

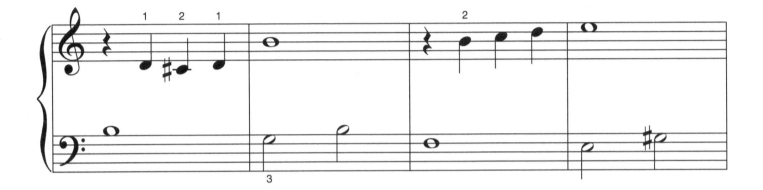

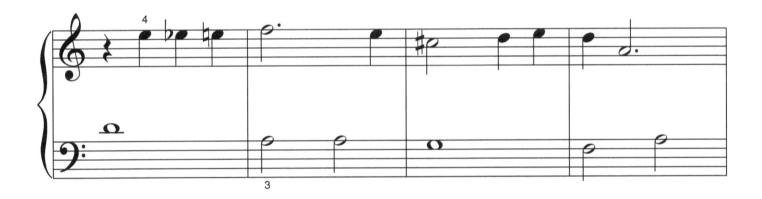

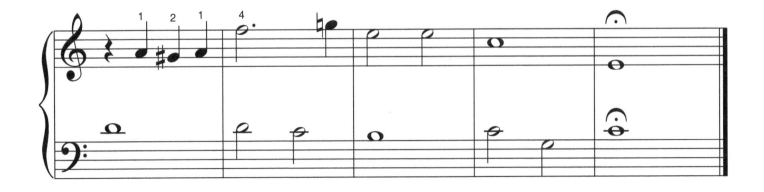

I'VE GROWN ACCUSTOMED TO HER FACE

from MY FAIR LADY

Words by ALAN JAY LERNER
Music by FREDERICK LOEWE

Gently

With pedal

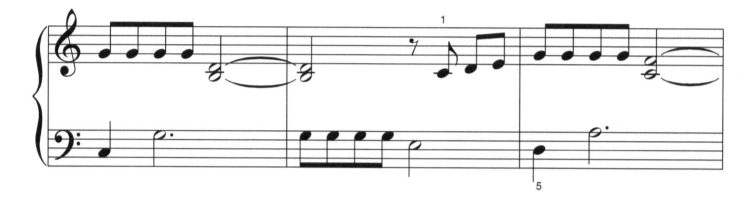

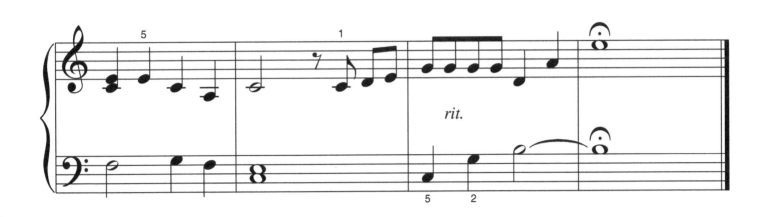

IN MY ROOM

Words and Music by BRIAN WILSON
and GARY USHER

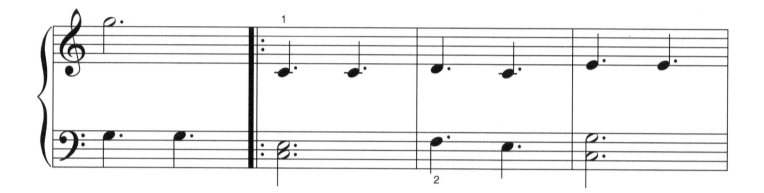

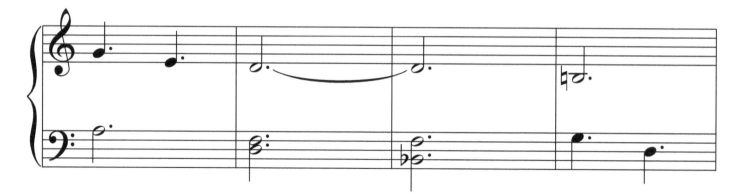

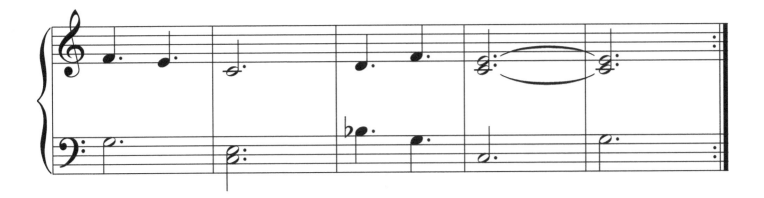

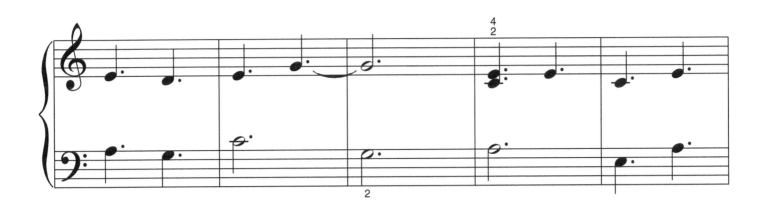

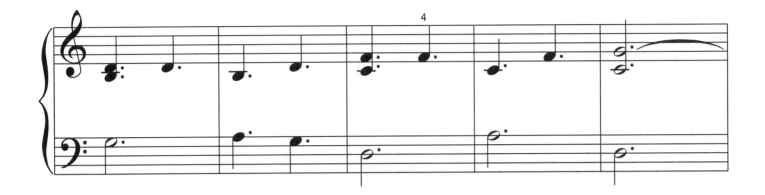

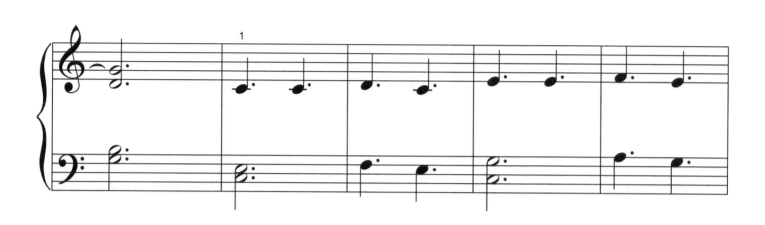

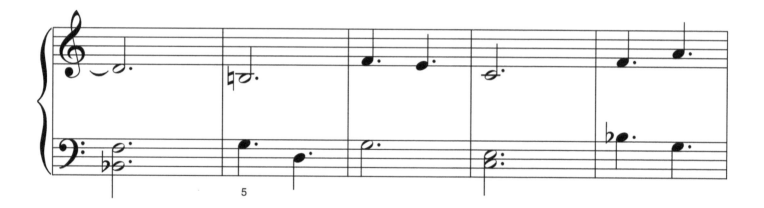

LOLLIPOPS AND ROSES

Words and Music by
TONY VELONA

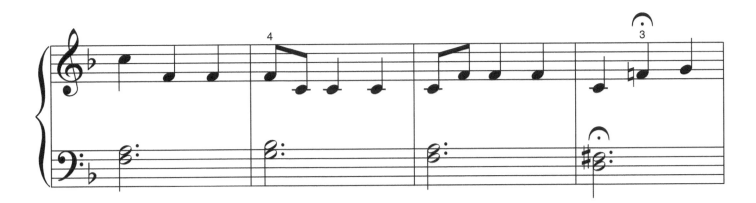

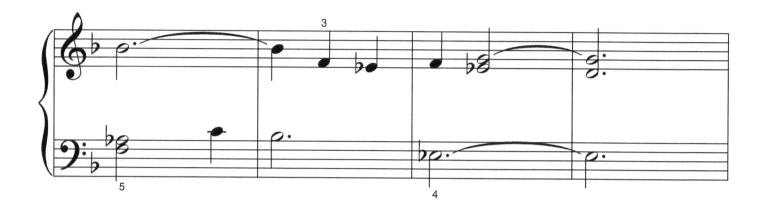

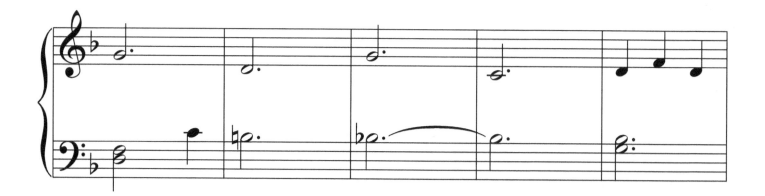

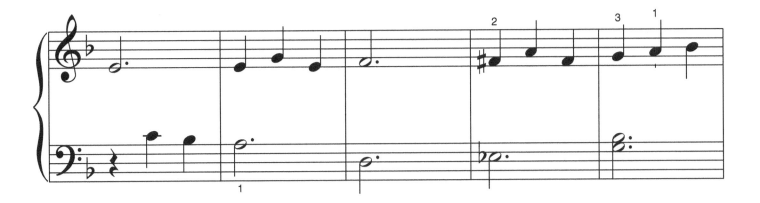

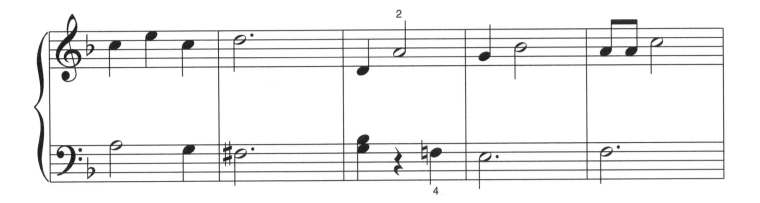

IN THE STILL OF THE NIGHT

from ROSALIE
from NIGHT AND DAY

Words and Music by
COLE PORTER

Moderately, in 2

mf

With pedal

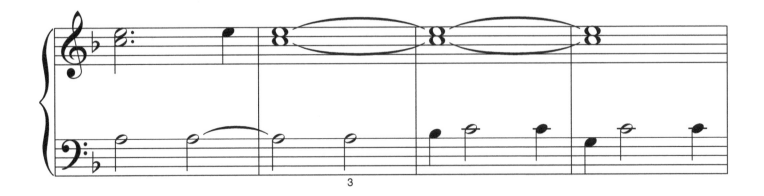

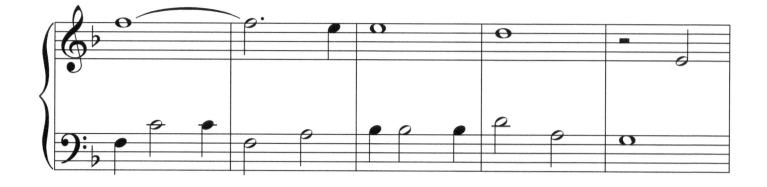

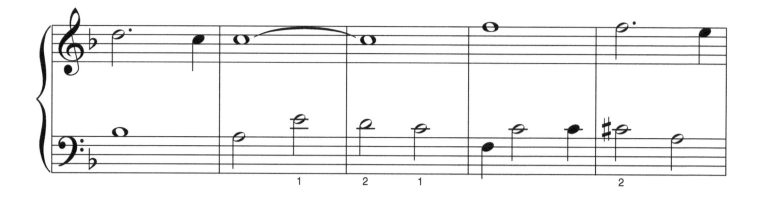

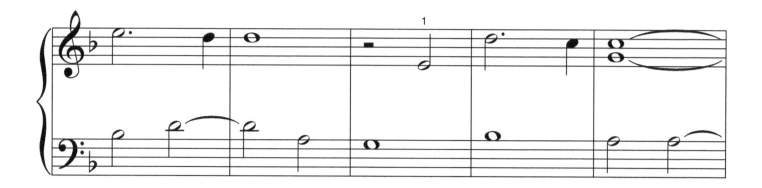

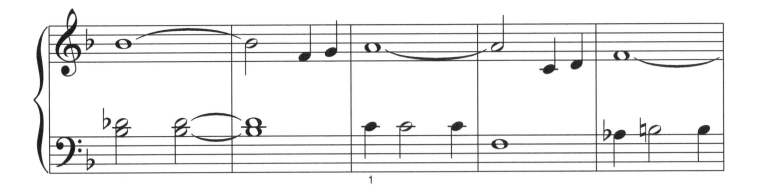

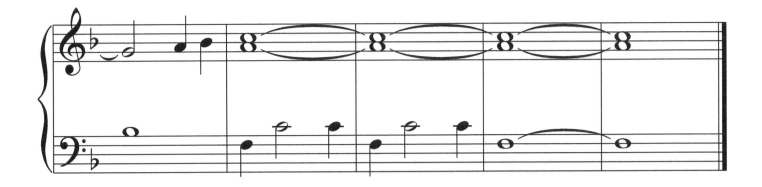

IN THE WEE SMALL HOURS OF THE MORNING

Words by BOB HILLIARD
Music by DAVID MANN

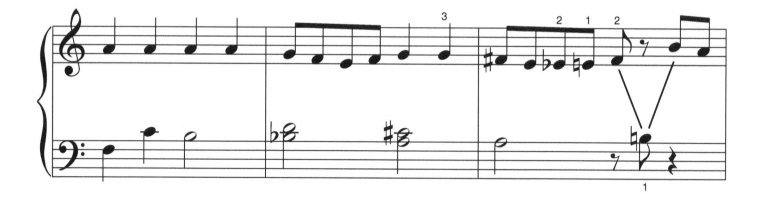

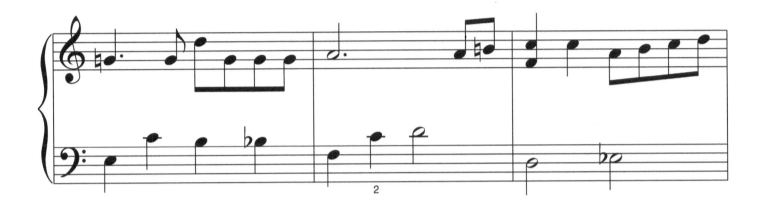

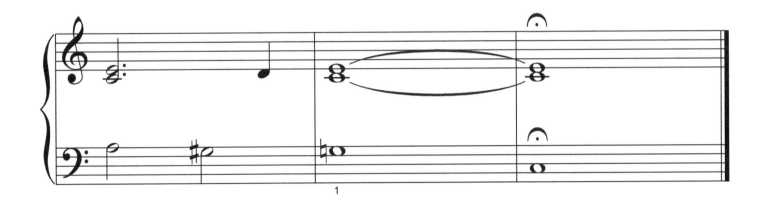

ISN'T IT ROMANTIC?
from the Paramount Picture LOVE ME TONIGHT

Words by LORENZ HART
Music by RICHARD RODGERS

Moderately

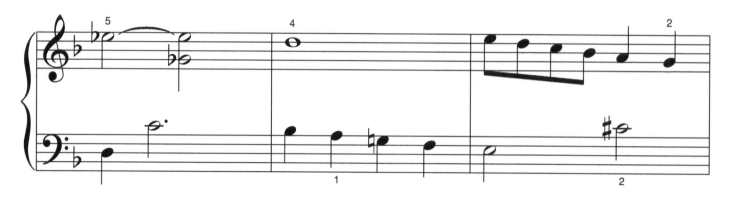

THE LAST TIME I SAW PARIS

from LADY, BE GOOD
from TILL THE CLOUDS ROLL BY

Lyrics by OSCAR HAMMERSTEIN II
Music by JEROME KERN

Moderately, in 2

LOVING YOU

Words and Music by JERRY LEIBER
and MIKE STOLLER

Moderately

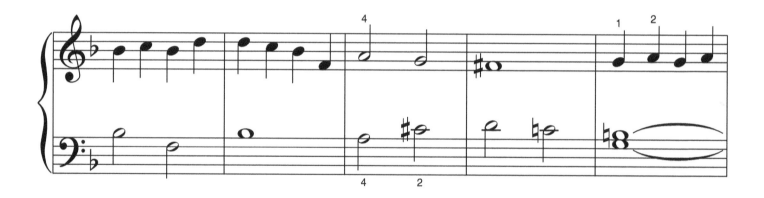

MEMORY
from CATS

Music by ANDREW LLOYD WEBBER
Text by TREVOR NUNN after T.S. ELIOT

Flowing, in one

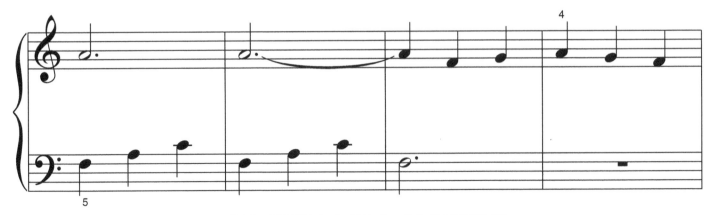

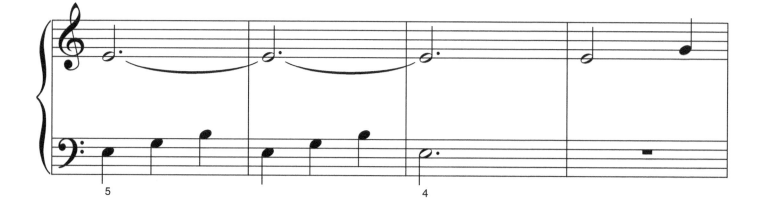

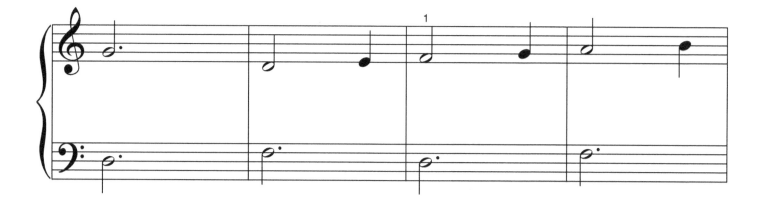

To Coda

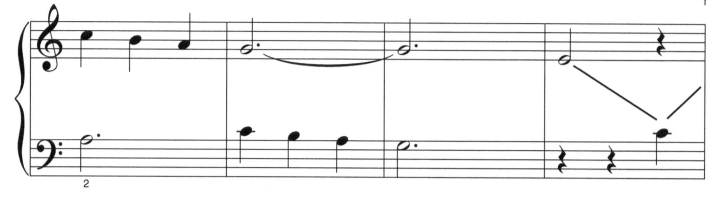

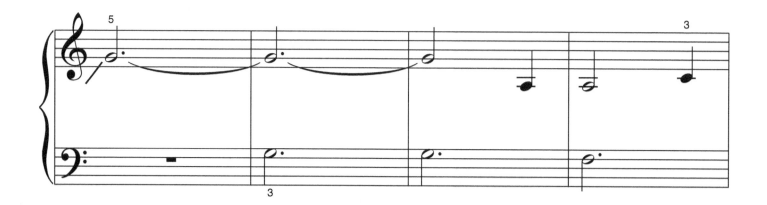

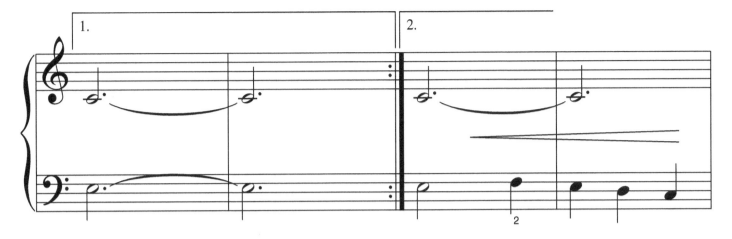

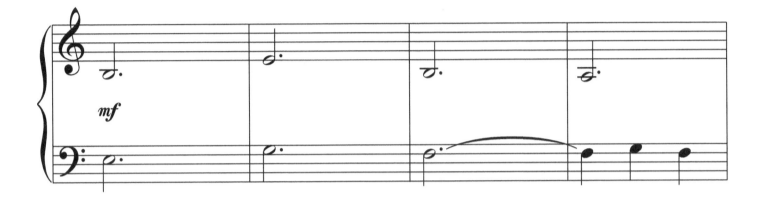

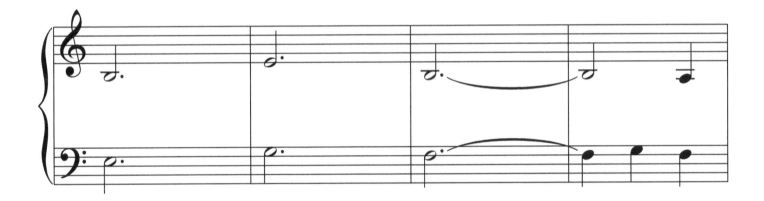

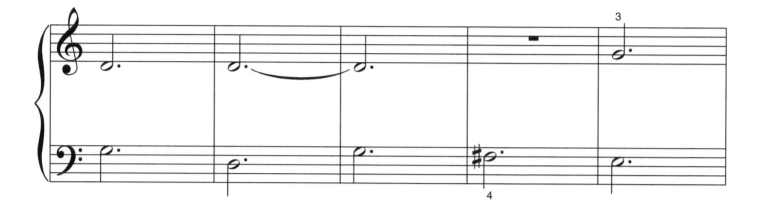

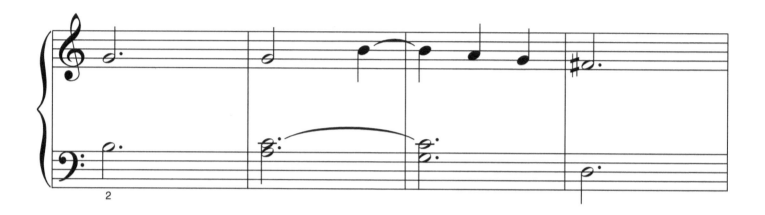

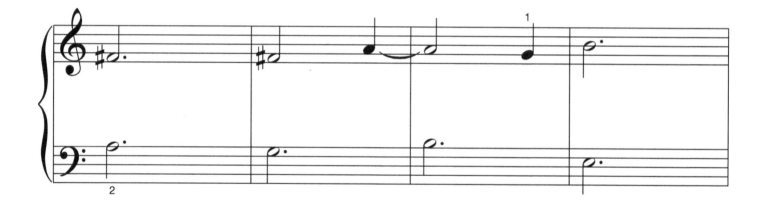

D.C. al Coda

CODA

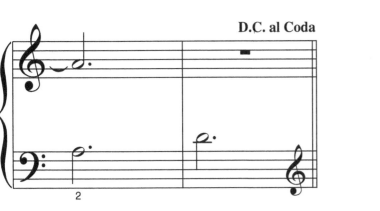

decresc.

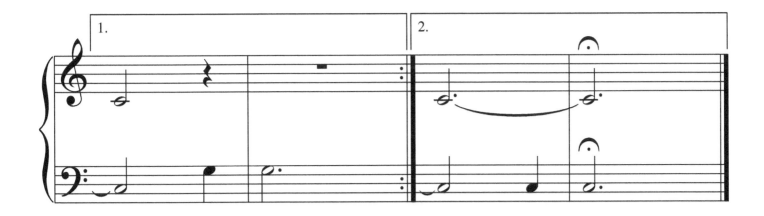

MOON RIVER

from the Paramount Picture BREAKFAST AT TIFFANY'S

Words by JOHNNY MERCER
Music by HENRY MANCINI

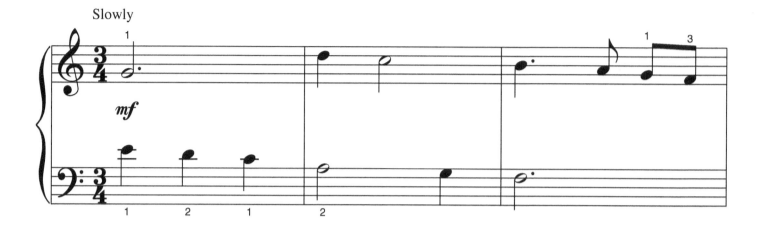

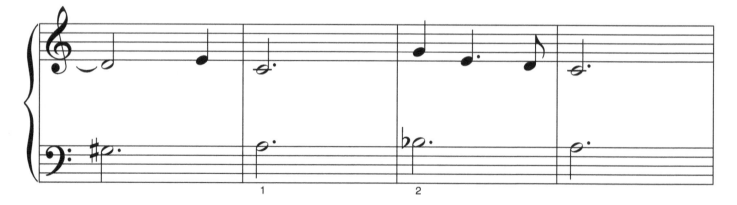

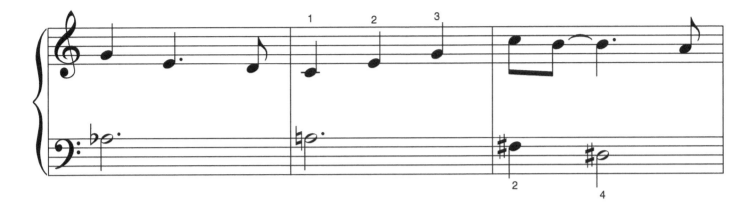

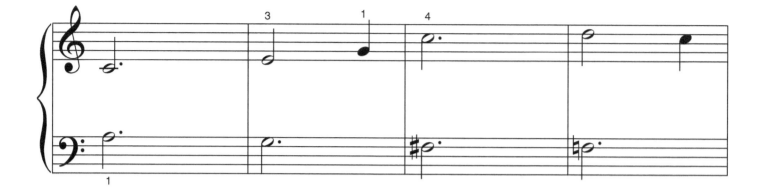

MY FUNNY VALENTINE
from BABES IN ARMS

Words by LORENZ HART
Music by RICHARD RODGERS

Slowly

With pedal

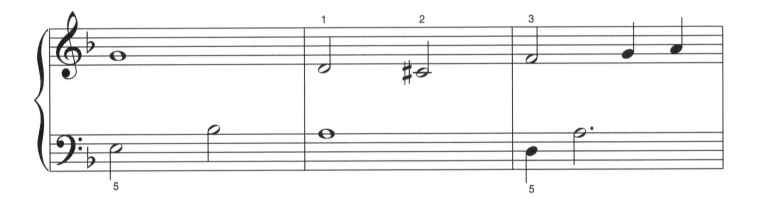

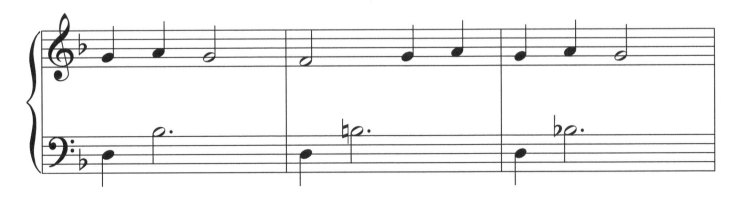

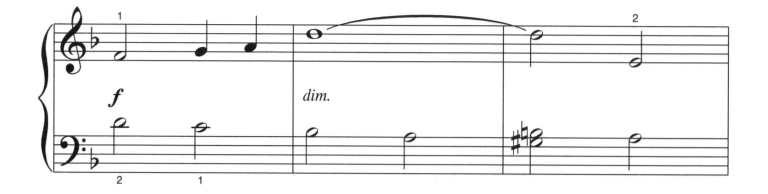

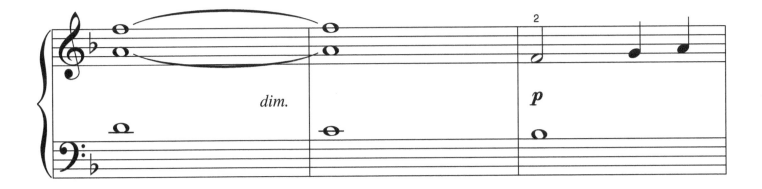

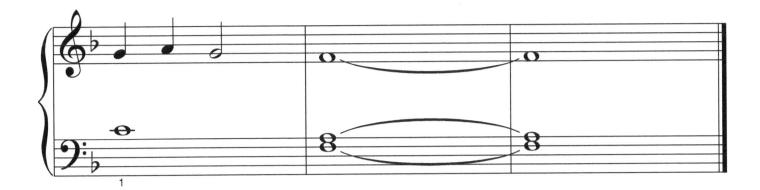

THE NEARNESS OF YOU

from the Paramount Picture ROMANCE IN THE DARK

Words by NED WASHINGTON
Music by HOAGY CARMICHAEL

Slowly

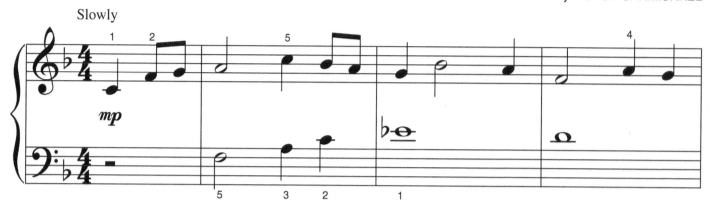

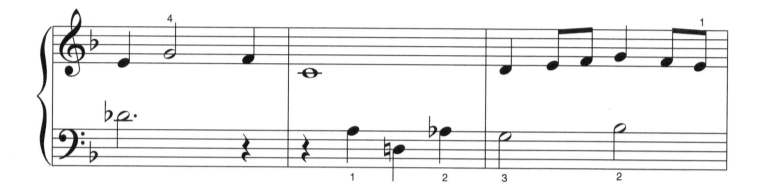

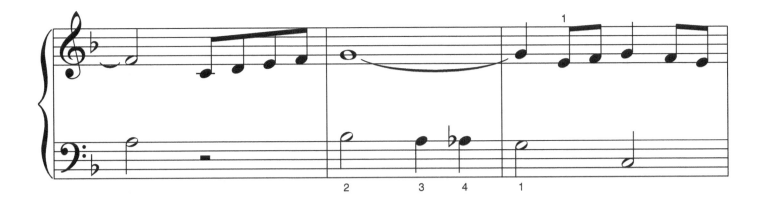

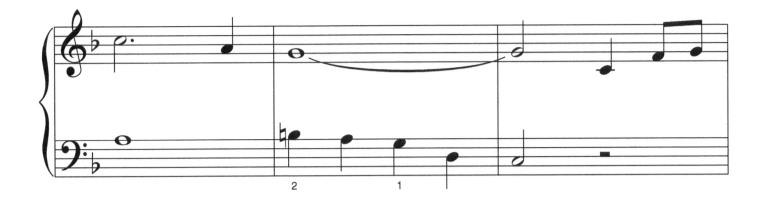

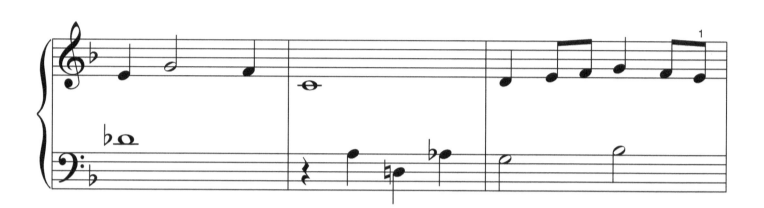

OH, WHAT A BEAUTIFUL MORNIN'
from OKLAHOMA!

Lyrics by OSCAR HAMMERSTEIN II
Music by RICHARD RODGERS

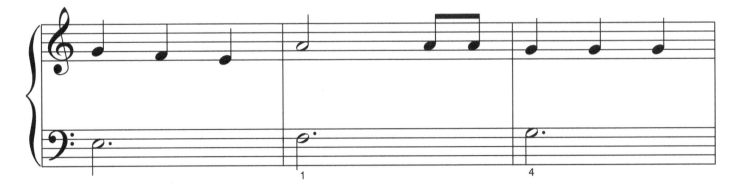

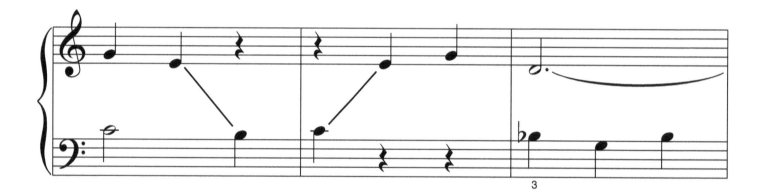

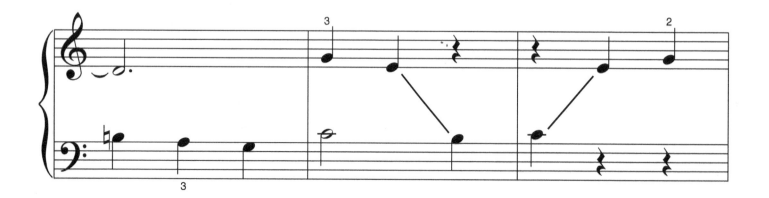

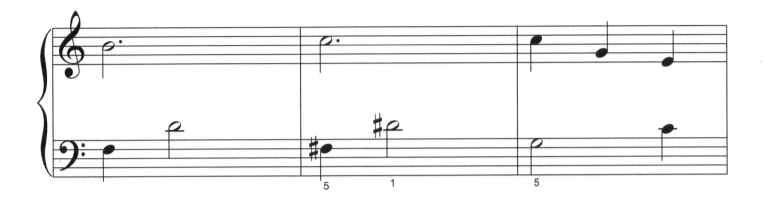

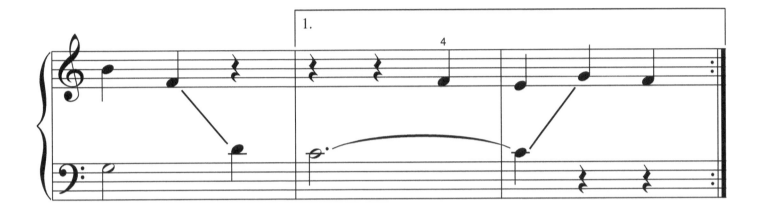

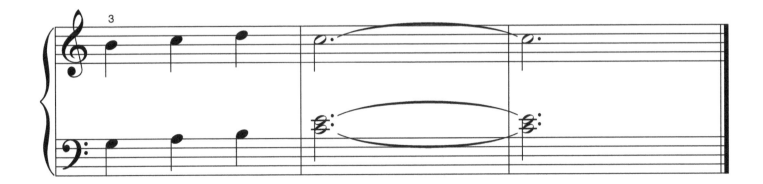

OVER THE RAINBOW

from THE WIZARD OF OZ

Music by HAROLD ARLEN
Lyric by E.Y. "YIP" HARBURG

Dreamily

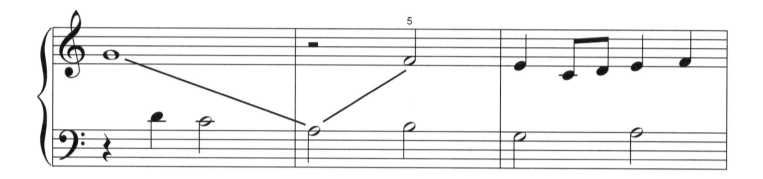

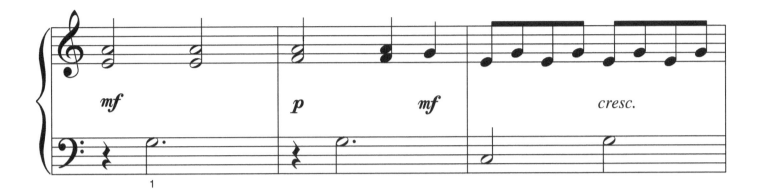

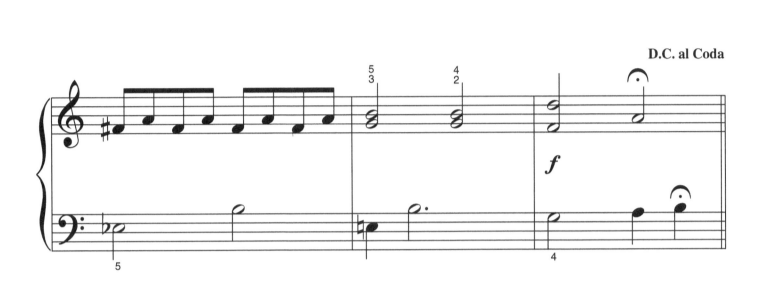

THE RAINBOW CONNECTION

from THE MUPPET MOVIE

Words and Music by PAUL WILLIAMS
and KENNETH L. ASCHER

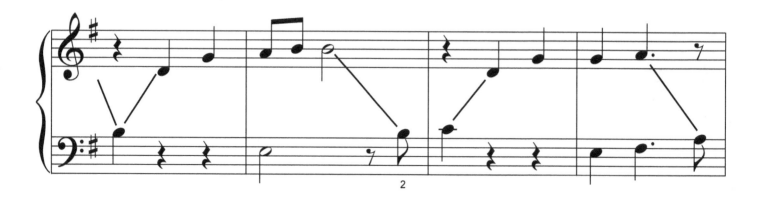

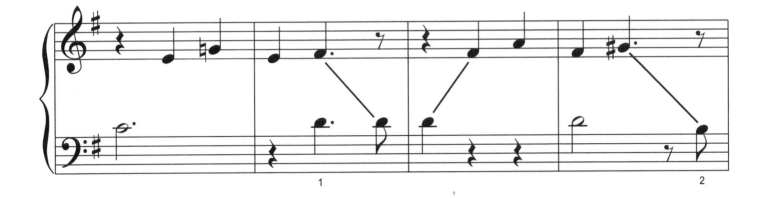

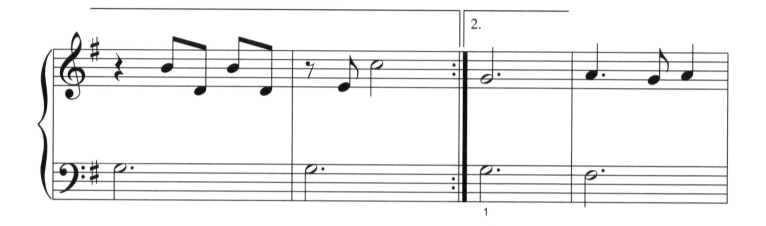

Release Me

Words and Music by ROBERT YOUNT,
EDDIE MILLER and DUB WILLIAMS

Moderately slow

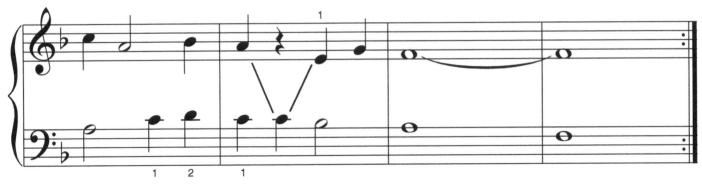

SINCERELY

Words and Music by ALAN FREED
and HARVEY FUQUA

SMILE

Words by JOHN TURNER
and GEOFFREY PARSONS
Music by CHARLES CHAPLIN

Slowly

With pedal

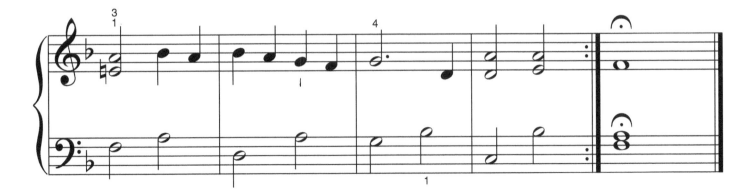

SMOKE GETS IN YOUR EYES

from ROBERTA

Words by OTTO HARBACH
Music by JEROME KERN

Slowly

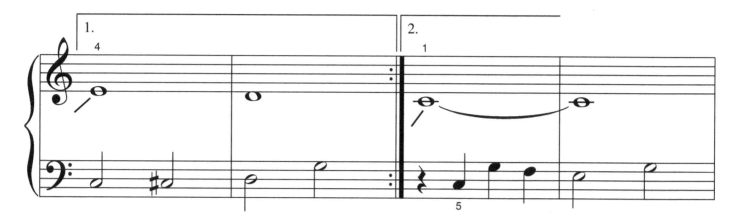

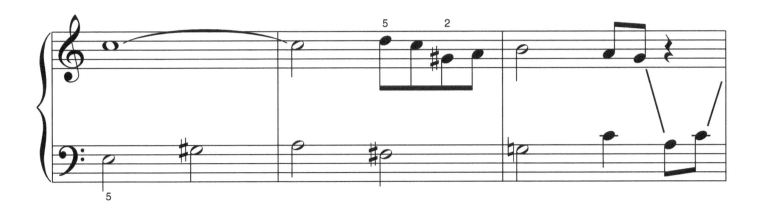

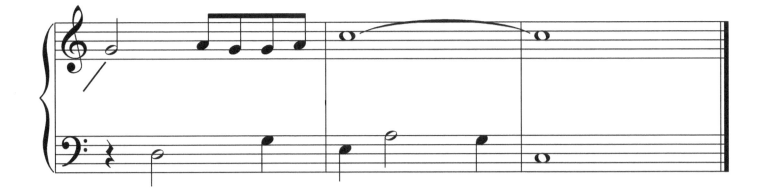

SO IN LOVE
from KISS ME, KATE

Words and Music by
COLE PORTER

Expressively, in 2

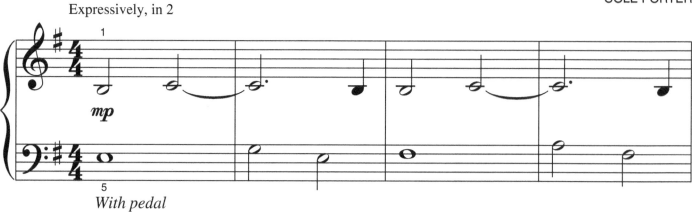

With pedal

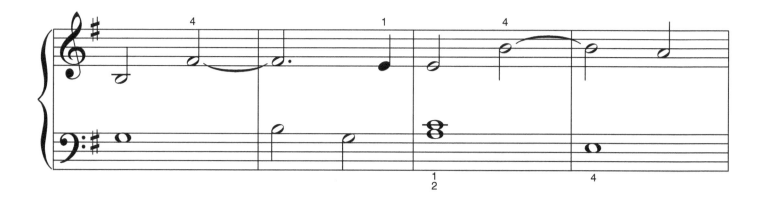

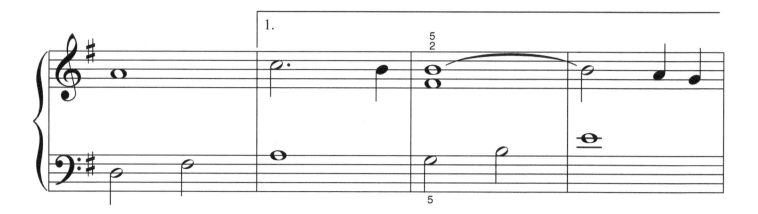

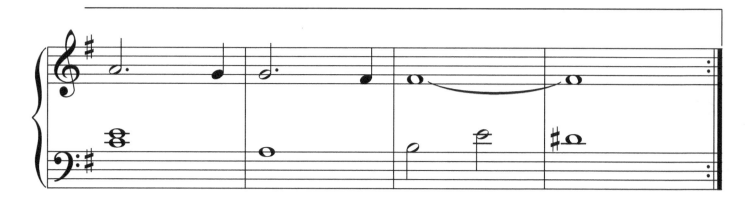

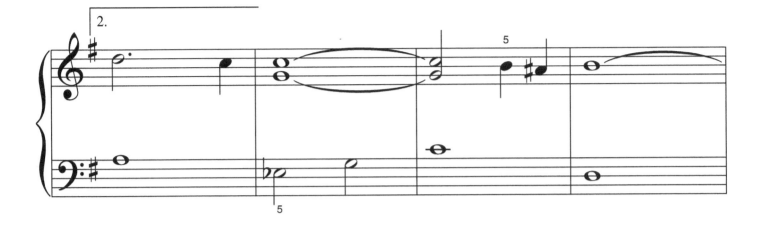

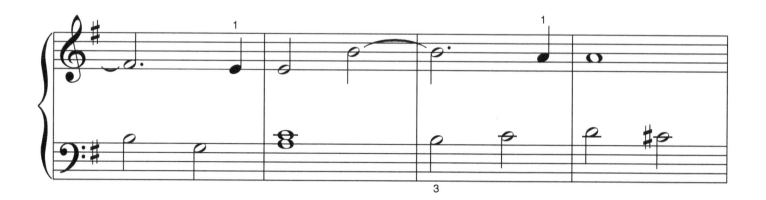

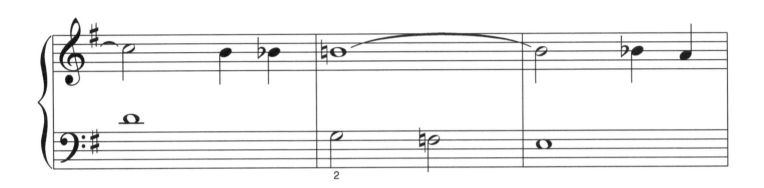

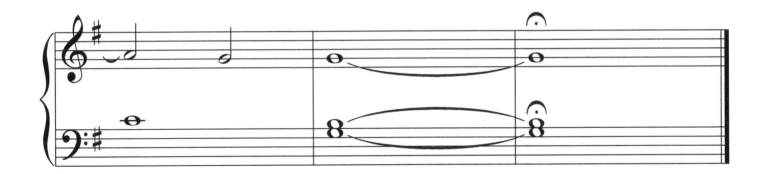

SOME DAY MY PRINCE WILL COME

Words by LARRY MOREY
Music by FRANK CHURCHILL

Slow Waltz

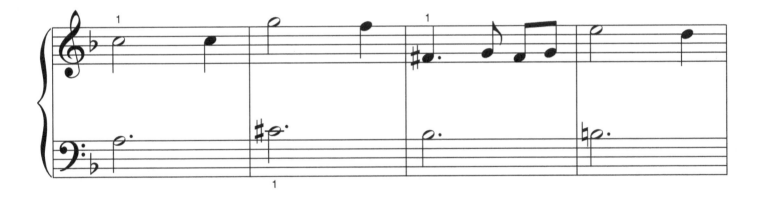

SOMEWHERE OUT THERE

from AN AMERICAN TAIL

Music by BARRY MANN
and JAMES HORNER
Lyric by CYNTHIA WEIL

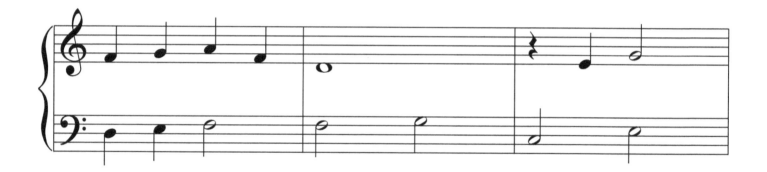

rit. a tempo

5

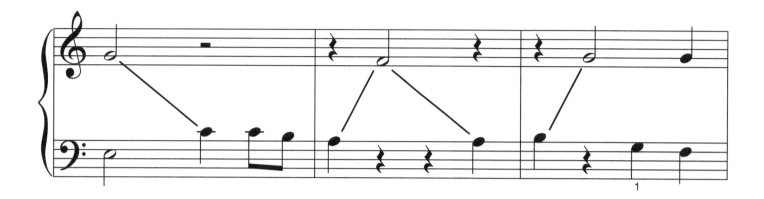

rit.

STRANGERS IN THE NIGHT
adapted from A MAN COULD GET KILLED

Words by CHARLES SINGLETON
and EDDIE SNYDER
Music by BERT KAEMPFERT

Moderately

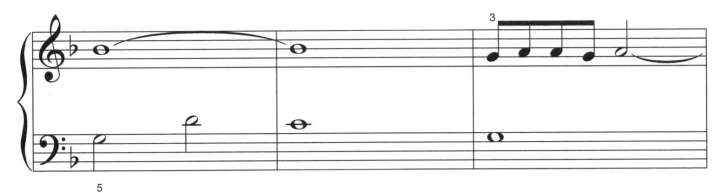

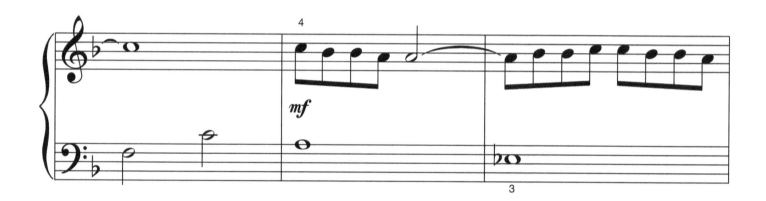

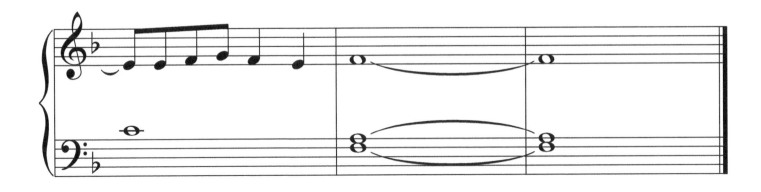

SPEAK SOFTLY, LOVE
(Love Theme)
from the Paramount Picture THE GODFATHER

Words by LARRY KUSIK
Music by NINO ROTA

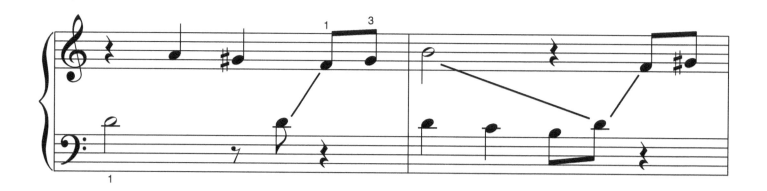

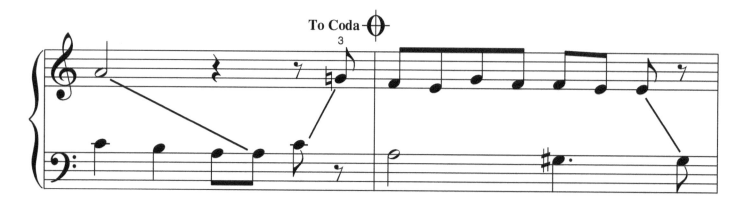

D.S. al Coda

CODA

TEARS IN HEAVEN

Words and Music by ERIC CLAPTON
and WILL JENNINGS

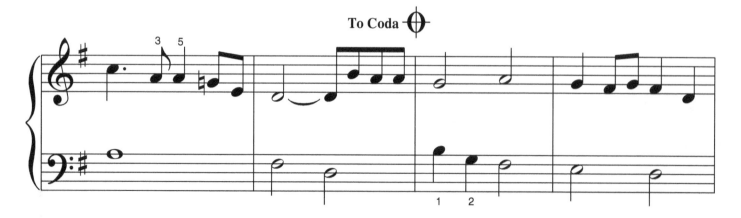

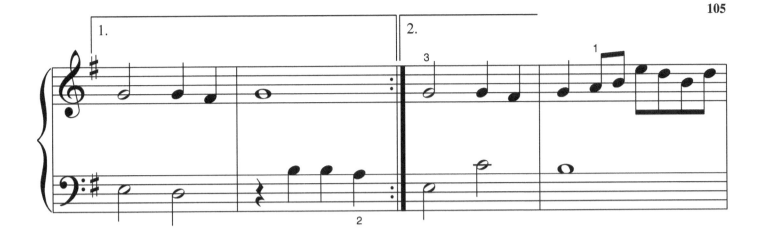

D.C. al Coda

CODA

TIME IN A BOTTLE

Words and Music by
JIM CROCE

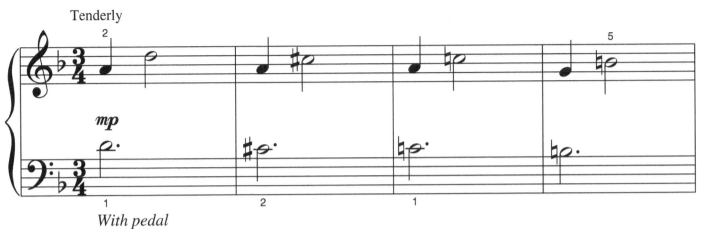

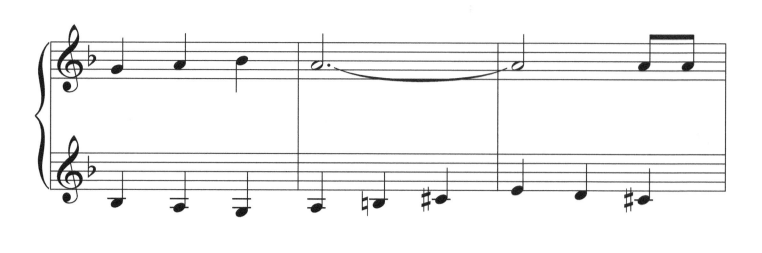

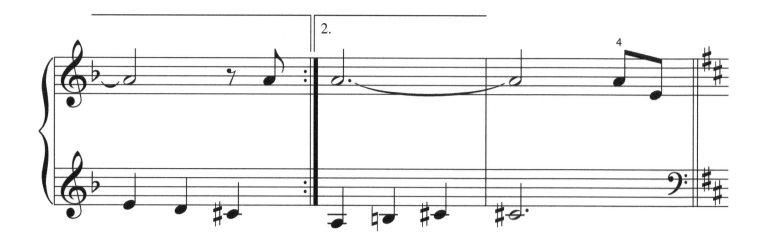

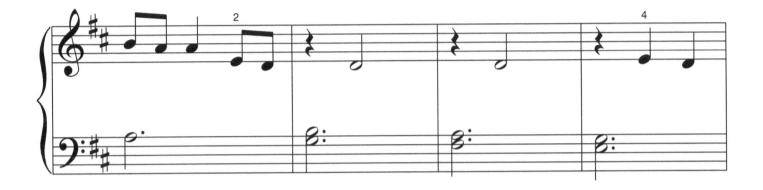

TENDERLY
from TORCH SONG

Lyric by JACK LAWRENCE
Music by WALTER GROSS

Slowly

With pedal

To Coda

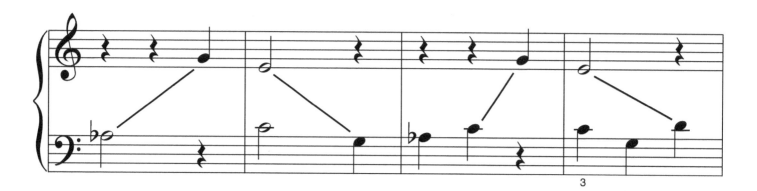

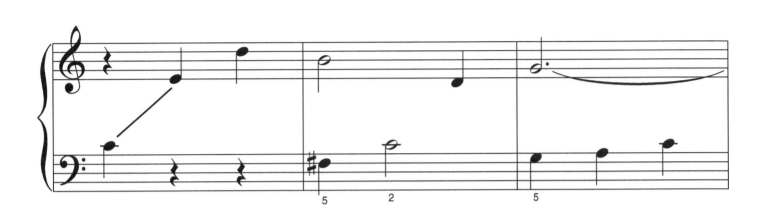

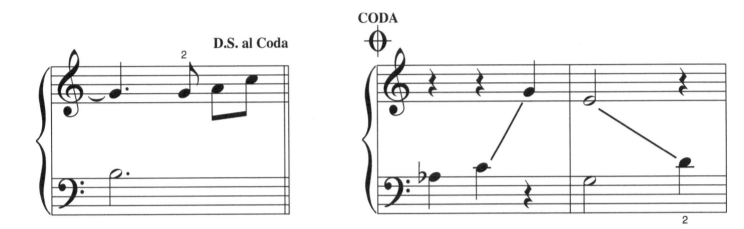

TRUE LOVE
from HIGH SOCIETY

Words and Music by
COLE PORTER

Moderately

With pedal

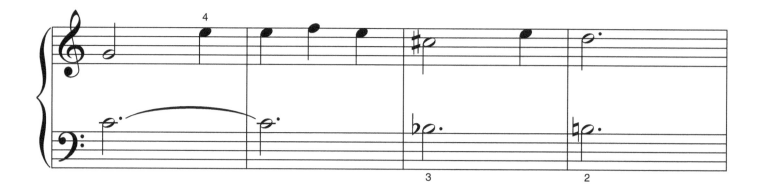

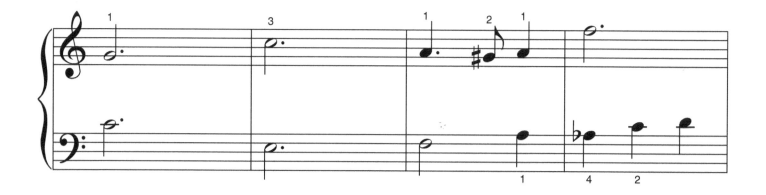

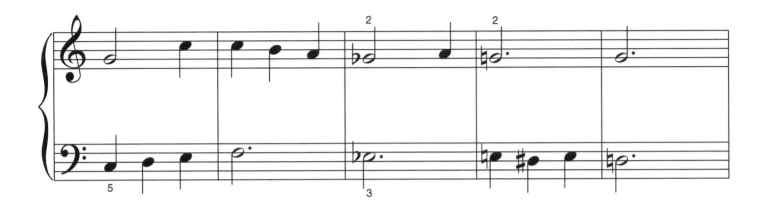

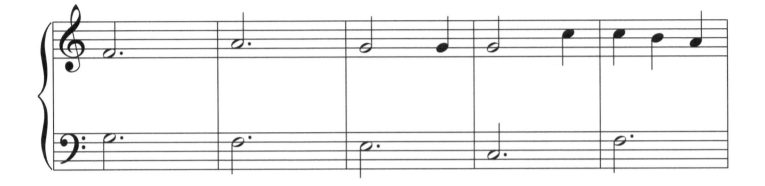

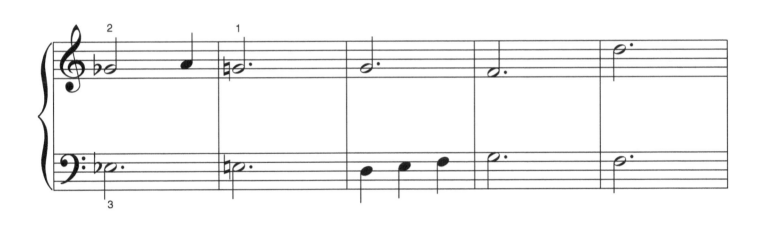

WHERE DO I BEGIN
(Love Theme)
from the Paramount Picture LOVE STORY

Words by CARL SIGMAN
Music by FRANCIS LAI

Slowly

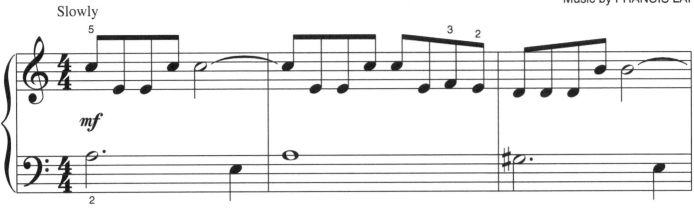

mf

With pedal

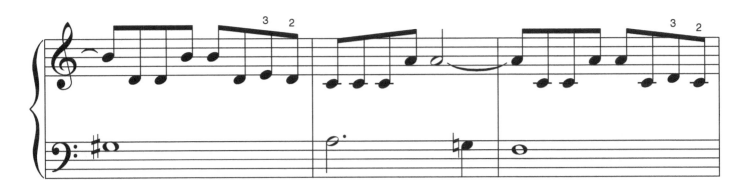

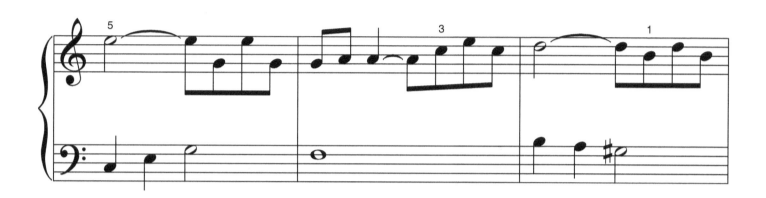

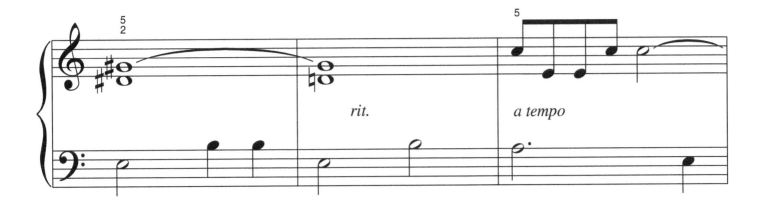

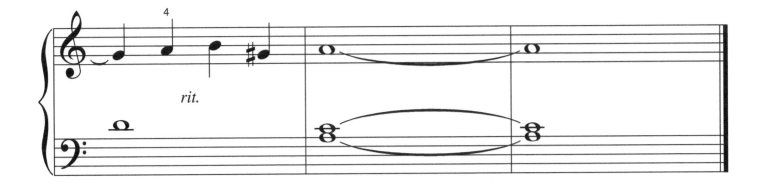

TRY TO REMEMBER
from THE FANTASTICKS

Words by TOM JONES
Music by HARVEY SCHMIDT

WHEN I FALL IN LOVE

from ONE MINUTE TO ZERO

Words by EDWARD HEYMAN
Music by VICTOR YOUNG

Slowly

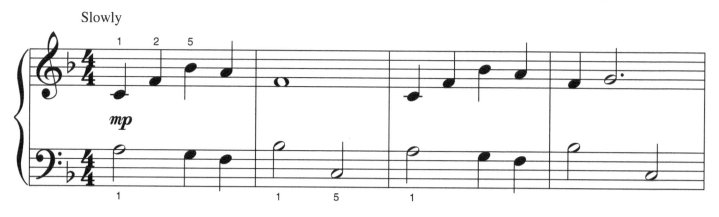

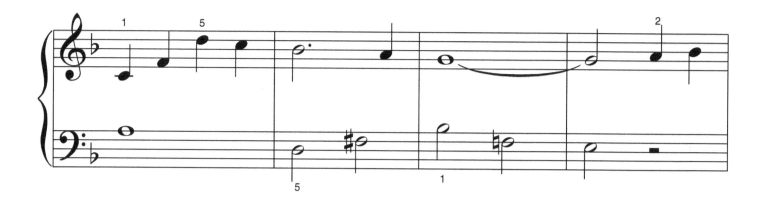

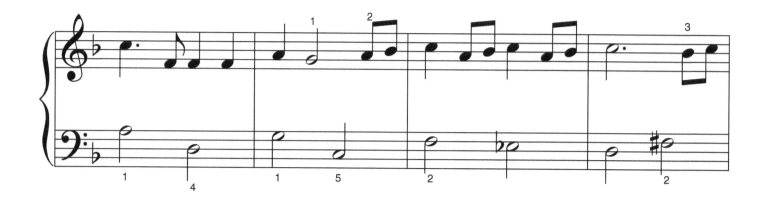

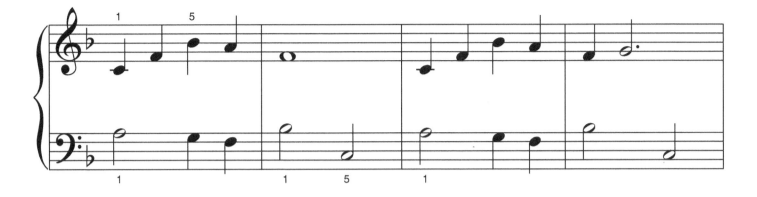

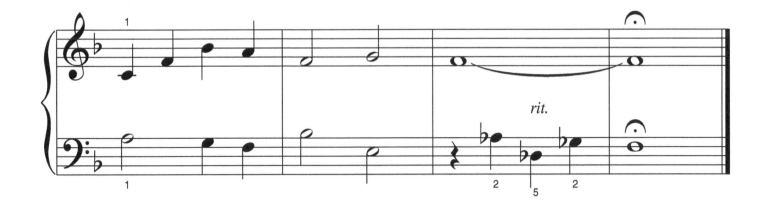

YESTERDAY

Words and Music by JOHN LENNON
and PAUL McCARTNEY

Slowly

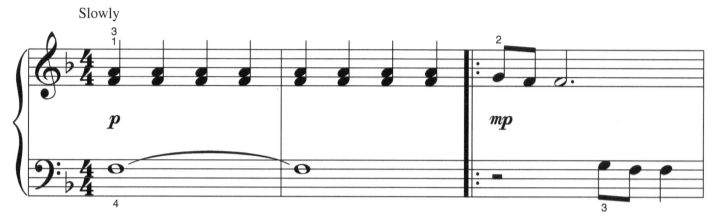

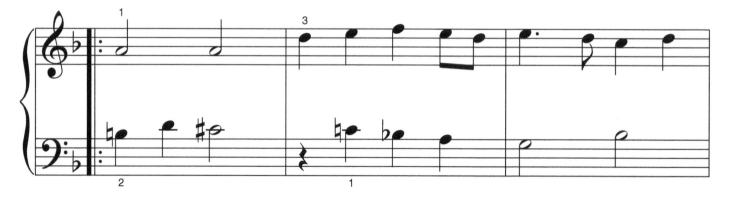

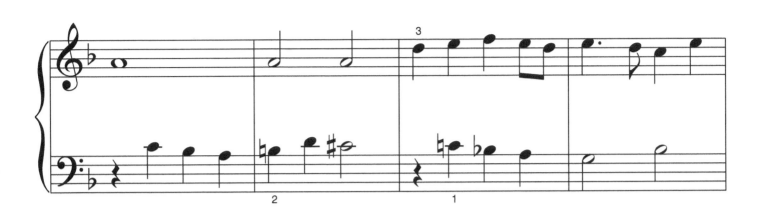

YOUNGER THAN SPRINGTIME

from SOUTH PACIFIC

Lyrics by OSCAR HAMMERSTEIN II
Music by RICHARD RODGERS

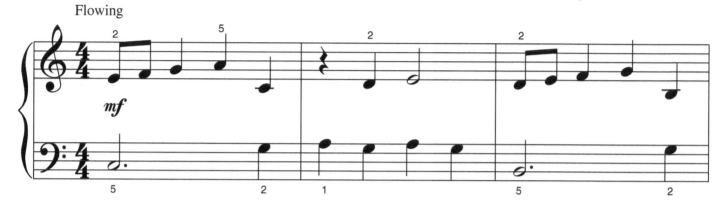

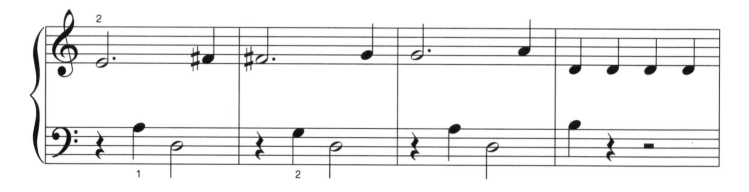

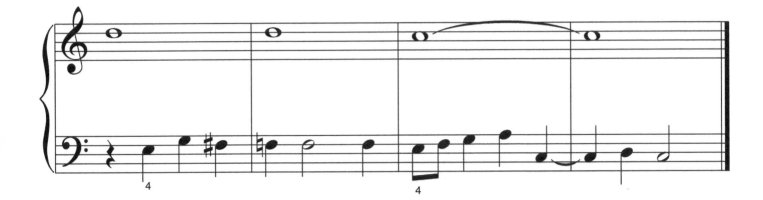

YOU LIGHT UP MY LIFE

Words and Music by
JOSEPH BROOKS

Moderately slow

mf

With pedal

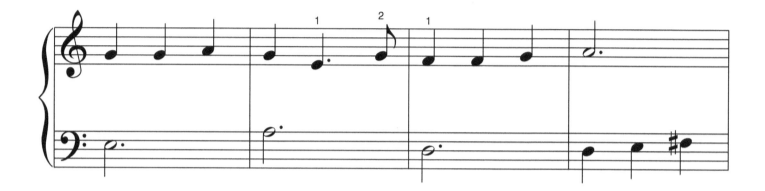

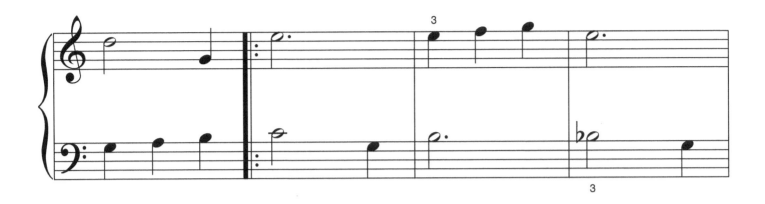

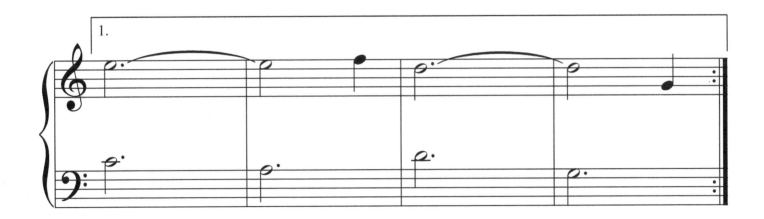